I0811532

# Pictures

by Wesley Dixon
illustrated by Bill Sheridan

Practice Pre-Decodable 12

McGraw Hill Education

Bothell, WA • Chicago, IL • Columbus, OH • New York, NY

**MHEonline.com**



Send all inquiries to:
McGraw-Hill Education
8787 Orion Place
Columbus, OH 43240

ISBN: 978-0-02-141256-3
MHID: 0-02-141256-1

Printed in China.

9 10 11 12 13 DSS 27 26 25 24 23

You see  and  .

mountains flowers

You see a  .

lake

You see a  .

boat

You see a .

fish

You see  and  .

Mom Dad

You see  .

pictures